THE PICAROONS.

THE PICAROONS;

or,

One Hundred and Fifty Years Ago

By

Richard Hill

The Black Heritage Library Collection

BOOKS FOR LIBRARIES PRESS

FREEPORT, NEW YORK

1971

First Published 1869
Reprinted 1971

F2161
H6

Reprinted from a copy in the
Fisk University Library Negro Collection

INTERNATIONAL STANDARD BOOK NUMBER:
0-8369-8943-0

LIBRARY OF CONGRESS CATALOG CARD NUMBER:
77-37306

PRINTED IN THE UNITED STATES OF AMERICA
BY
NEW WORLD BOOK MANUFACTURING CO., INC.
HALLANDALE, FLORIDA 33009

THE PICAROONS;

OR,

One Hundred and Fifty Years Ago:

BEING A

HISTORY OF COMMERCE AND NAVIGATION

IN

THE WEST INDIAN SEAS.

BY

THE HONORABLE RICHARD HILL.

"Nihil scriptum miraculi causâ."—*Tacitus.*

COMMUNICATED TO THE PORT ROYAL READING SOCIETY.

DUBLIN:
JOHN FALCONER, 53, UPPER SACKVILLE-STREET,
PRINTER TO HER MAJESTY'S STATIONERY OFFICE.

1869.

DUBLIN: JOHN FALCONER, 53, UPPER SACKVILLE-STREET.

TO

SIR JOHN P. GRANT, K.C.B.,

GOVERNOR AND CAPTAIN-GENERAL OF JAMAICA,
AND ITS DEPENDENCIES,
ETC., ETC., ETC.

DEAR SIR JOHN,

I have much pleasure in availing myself of your kind permission to dedicate this little work to you. Jamaica was the principal theatre of the events it records, and therefore the propriety of my having solicited this favour is obvious.

Allow me to remind you that the manuscript was presented, through me, to the Port Royal Literary and Mechanics' Institution (which I was instrumental in establishing last year), from my excellent friend, the Honorable Richard Hill, of Spanish Town, its talented author. When I suggested to him that the utility of his valuable contribution would be largely increased if allowed to appear in print, he at once most generously placed the MS. at my entire disposal, to make any use of it I thought might be most conducive to the benefit of the above Institution, which has for its sole object the mental cultivation and literary amusement of the working classes of Port Royal; and to its support will be devoted any profits arising from the sale of the work.

I remain, my Dear Sir John,
Faithfully yours,

F. L. M'CLINTOCK,
Late Commodore at Jamaica.

DUBLIN, 21, MERRION-SQUARE, NORTH,
16th October, 1868.

THE PICAROONS;

OR,

One Hundred and Fifty Years Ago.

THE piratical warfare, carried on in the West Indian Seas immediately after Columbus's discovery, was the result of the exclusive navigation to the Continent and Islands assumed by the Spaniards. The non-compliance of mariners with a right maintainable only by mastery, gave rise to the Fraternity of Freebooters, known as the Buccaneers—composed of Englishmen, Frenchmen, and Dutchmen.

The Buccaneers divided their time on the Island of Hispaniola, where they had gained a footing from their stronghold Tortuga—between hunting wild cattle on shore, and pillaging vessels at sea. They boucané-ed, or sun-dried, after the Indian fashion, the flesh of the cattle they killed, using a word for the process from *Boucan*, an open kitchen, where they dressed the slaughtered beeves. Their hunting grounds are to be traced on the maps of Haiti, as the Grand Boucan, the Boucan-bron, and Boucassoir.

There is no description of these Sea-Rovers so graphic and condensed as that given by Mr. Charles Waterton in his record of a visit to the Island of St.

Thomas, in the first journey of his *Wanderings*.
"At St. Thomas's," he says, "they show you a tower,
a little distance from the town, which they say formerly
belonged to a Buccanier* chieftain; probably the fury
of besiegers has reduced it to its present dismantled
state. What still remains of it bears testimony to its
former strength, and may brave the attack of time for
centuries. You cannot view its ruins without calling
to mind the exploits of those fierce and hardy hunters,
long the terror of the Western World. While you
admire their undaunted courage, you lament that it was
often stained with cruelty ; while you extol their scrupulous justice to each other, you will find a want of it
towards the rest of mankind. Often possessed of
wealth, often in extreme poverty, often triumphant on
the ocean, and often forced to fly to the forests ; their
life was an ever-changing scene of advance and retreat,
of glory and disorder, of luxury and famine. Spain
treated them as outlaws and pirates, while other
European powers publicly disowned them. They, on
the other hand, maintained that injustice on the part
of Spain first forced them to take up arms in self-
defence; and that whilst they kept inviolable the laws
which they had framed for their own common benefit
and protection, they had a right to consider as foes,
those who treated them as outlaws. Under this im-
pression they drew the sword, and rushed on as though
in lawful war, and divided the spoils of victory in the
scale of justice."

* Waterton spells the word as above. The true writing of the name
should be Bouccanier; the spelling, however, ordinarily, is Buccaneer.

When Cromwell's expedition gave Jamaica to England by conquest, the Buccaneers had a port to which
they could resort with confident assurance of recognition and protection. The acquisition of Jamaica was
the first breaking ground with Spain in national warfare in the New World. Portugal, under the bull of
Pope Alexander the Sixth, divided the South American
Continent with Spain. She had supported herself in
her revolt from the peninsular power by the war that
France and Holland had waged with Spain. On the
restoration of Charles II. to the English throne, his
marriage with a princess of the House of Braganza
gave him influence with Spain to induce the abandonment of the claim to the Portuguese kingdom. Contending interests were tranquillized in Europe, but
exclusive maritime pretences remained as they had
been, a source of conflicts and aggression in the
waters of America. James, Duke of York, the King's
brother, was Lord High Admiral of England. He
constituted his Admiralty Court in Jamaica. Commissions were issued to frigates and private ships to
"prey upon the neighbouring territories and make
prizes at sea," as the license phrased it; and it made
known that no adventurers would be allowed, but such
as were authorized by powers, as the King's ordinance
expressed it, "from our dearest brother, the Duke of
York." There was peace in the Old World; but war,
under the worst species of warfare—a war of enterprize
and retaliation—was waged in the seas of the New
World.

While Spain was a common enemy, all went swimmingly on among Englishmen, Frenchmen, and Dutchmen, with an occasional Dane making a dash at pillage. We shall see that the abdication of James II. and the elevation of William and Mary to the throne of England gave a special turn to hostilities. The French declared themselves armed on the ocean, not against England, but against England's Government. Pedro and Juan, the successive Kings of Portugal, had joined the grand confederacy formed by King William against Louis XIV. In 1707, Marlborough had conquered at Ramillies, and was winning the battle of Oudenarde, when the King of Portugal had nearly ruined the allies of England by the loss of the fight of Almanza. The vast shores of Brazil, however, were secure Asylums to the belligerents against France and Spain in the Atlantic Ocean; and buccaneering became, by the disputed throne of England, legitimate undertakings for English subjects against the English flag. An adventurer could be a friend and an enemy, when Frenchmen, Englishmen, and Dutchmen were no longer confederates. War was a game played by each commander of an armed ship, for himself alone. Freebootering— or, as foreigners mis-pronounce it, fillibustering— at this period, until the accession of the House of Hanover, became not so much the bold hazard of the Buccaneer as the piracy of the Picaroon.

In 1700 we arrive at the incidents of the Picaroon period. The ultimate issue of maritime contentions in the West Indies, we are about to give under the title of " One Hundred and Fifty Years Ago." The sequel of the long series of conflicts with Spain became eventually the Revolutions that freed Central. and Southern America from their dependency on Europe.

From 1692, the year of the great earthquake of Port Royal, to 1722, the year of the great storm, disastrous visitations, appointed by the legislature of Jamaica to be kept in remembrance perpetually as fast days, and days of humiliation, the colony suffered constantly from the pillage of Picaroons. A system of retaliatory plundering had been organized by the national Colonists, Frenchmen, and Spaniards, and Englishmen, leagued with Dutchmen. The sea-board plantations were the objects of pillage, and the most brutal outrages were perpetrated by one upon the other. Dashes at the settlements had a profitable purpose in the carrying away of negro slaves. If it was worth while to go to Africa to bring negroes into the Colonies, and to enslave them, it was more profitable to steal them from the Colonies, when they were already there.

Jamaica in 1696 had passed a law which enjoined masters to instruct their enslaved dependents in Christianity. The act required them, " not to fail to exhort all male and female slaves who may be unbaptized to receive the sacrament of Baptism." At that time the sentiment prevailed that Christians could not be made slaves. It was only Pagans that were reducible to bondage : infidels alone could lawfully be subject to slavery. The reception of enslaved unbelievers into the bosom of the Church would be virtual enfranchisement. The law therefore which enjoined the duty of exhorting slaves to be baptized, enacted that "no slave shall be free by becoming Christian." Man manifested a right knowledge, but acted by a wrong principle. They adopted the maxim, "evil be thou my good." God takes man on his own terms. He desires to be left to his own evil heart, and in his evil devices he becomes a demon. The inspired Volume represents human life as a dream that passes fleeting away, leaving its remembrance as a tale that is told. Inconstant as a vapour, it assumes one form to vanish in another. It flourishes as a flower in the morning, and is cut down in the evening and withered. The active spirit of the colony was to make the most of it by sensual enjoyment : " Let us eat and drink, for to-morrow we die." Revelation was for the slave. The hopeless bondman was not to die hopelessly. Life might be misery in its drag of daily toil. Housed and fed, his human strength was to be nourished for labour. There was to be no future in time; no hope in life : futurity was the expectation of another world. He was to look forward to death for blessedness. His existence was to be a life of suffering. We constantly quote Job's consolatory thought of death, as a sleep of quietness, " where the wicked cease from troubling; where the weary are at rest." But we stop short, and never go on to the comforting thought that follows in the text, of the " prisoners resting together, and the servant being free from his master." (Book of Job, chap. iii., v. 17, 18, 19.) The slave's teaching was to be, a looking to death with the expectation of blessedness. He was to learn in a state of being that might have no want—but be without superabundance—the lesson of his great deliverer, " I am thy salvation." In unmitigable bondage—his own and his children's inheritance—he looked on the world of his master as one in which man acted as if there was nothing beyond the past and the present, and this exhibition of a practical disbelief of an hereafter, was to be comforted *in him*, by a Christian's hope in the future.

At the moment of the earthquake on the 7th of June, 1692, two hundred and ninety Buccaneers from St. Domingo, under one Daviot, were engaged plundering on the North side of Jamaica. One hundred and thirty-five were in St. Ann's Bay, in the act of carrying off fifty-two plantation Africans. For fifteen days, the marauders had been detained on shore. A gale of wind had driven off their vessel from the coast. Alarmed at the earthquake, they took their boats to gain their ship at sea. In the paroxysms of the shocks some were swamped; fifty-three of the crew were swallowed up. Those who escaped reached their vessel only to be encountered by cruisers off Cuba, sent to clear the coast of Daviot. In the action that ensued the Buccaneer ship was blown up, and Daviot perished. Twenty-one of the crew picked up were saved. Those of the pillaging party on shore surrendered, and were sent to St. Domingo.

Two years passed and Jamacia was revisited in the midst of the distress consequent on the earthquake. Pestilence and famine, had been upon them *within*, and the sword was now upon them from *without*. Du Cassé, an admiral of the French navy, commanded an expedition of three men of war, and twenty privateers, and landed one thousand five hundred troops. This was that Du Cassé who, eight years after, combating with the brave Admiral Benbow, in his mortal fight, wrote to him this complimentary letter after the spirit of the times. "Sir, I had little hope on Monday last but to have supped in your cabin; it pleased God to order otherwise. I am thankful for it. As for those cowardly captains who deserted you, hang them up, for by God they deserve it. Yours, Du Cassé." The two captains he referred to were Kirby and Wood. Du Cassé was off Santa Martha, having on board the Duke of Albuquerque on his way to Mexico, and commanded a squadron of four sail of the line and six smaller vessels. The encounter with Benbow became a running fight, lasting five days. Benbow, lying on the deck of his vessel, the Breda, with his leg shattered by a chain shot, was still determined to fight, but the two captains whom Du Cassé charged with cowardice, dissuaded their comrades from all further combat, with their force, seven sail of battle ships, though inferior to Du Cassé in metal. The brave Benbow, carried into Kingston, where he died, wrote his wife that "*the lop of his leg,*" as he expressed himself for the loss of his limb, "did not trouble him half so much as the villainous treachery of his captains." They were tried, convicted of cowardice, and shot. Du Cassé, with God's name in his mouth, but with nothing of God in his heart, perpetrated enormities from Cow Bay to Morant on the south side, in which the settlers, tortured to disclose their money, were made to behold their wives violated, and their slaves seized to the number of two thousand for shipment as prize. Both men and women were murdered. One of the most notorious of the demons associated with Du Cassé was De Graff, a well known Buccaneer, and the records of the time represent Beauregard, the ancestor of the late renowned confederate Chieftain of the rebel war of North America, as in command of the soldiers engaged, in harrying Jamaica under the desolation of the earthquake. Commodore Wilmot was sent to retaliate for these outrages by blowing up the fortress of Cape François, where De Graff's wife and two children were made prisoners. Known to be "a man's wife," though the wife of such a man as De Graff, she was treated with respect. This woman, De Graff had married because she had resented an insult to her person, by placing a pistol to his head and threatening him with death. De Graff declared that a woman of such a spirit was the only person worthy to be the wife of De Graff, and he then and there married her. (*Charluny's History*, Vol. iv., p. 57).

CHAPTER II.

IN an account of the "Rise and Growth of the West Indian Colonies," published by Dalby Thomas, in 1670,* it is said half the quantity of the shipping then afloat in the American trade, was occupied in predatory cruising against Spanish plate ships. Wealth was to be picked up by rapine; and Drake, Hawkins, Raleigh, and Clifford, precursors of the Buccaneers

* Harleian Miscellany, Vol. ix., p. 403-443.

found followers in numbers. The hostilities of Philip II. against Queen Elizabeth, and the pretensions of Spain to the throne of England, made all maritime plundering of Spanish commerce lawful. The rapacity of the many, was wrought upon by the example and success of the few. A war waged without design, help, or assistance, from State Councils, made England a maritime nation. When the elevation of the Prince of Orange to the English throne raised Holland to be a dominant power, the revolt of the Netherlanders from the Spanish dominion under the Duke of Alva, had settled their traditions into sworn hatred for the Spaniard. When the grasp made by Philip II. on Portugal aggrandized the Dutch in the East by making them commercial at the expense of the Portuguese, new vigour was given to the privateersman. Support to the abdicated James, against the successful occupation of the kingdom by William and Mary, had divided the allegiance of the people of England, while Holland, by her Oriental possessions, was practically a great power. Where profit was more esteemed than principle, and gain than honour, few scruples interposed against disputes with Dutchmen, who—cool and thrifty as they were, and cautious against offending—were held to be only honest by the discipline of trade and business. Out of that discipline they were esteemed rapacious under the guise of habits of frugality and diligence. Homage and fealty sat very loosely on Englishmen; among Irishmen, under difference of race and religion, they had no place, and among loyal Scotsmen, they only waited an opportunity to declare for the exiled Stuart. Dutch William had few adherents on the ocean beside Hollanders. The success that had made him a King by a Protestant wind, might unmake him in a Catholic storm, and the Freebooter was at sea, with a French license for any turn of fortune. He was safe proclaiming devotion to James against William, and as safe in alleging himself a partizan of William against James.

We shall content ourselves with exhibiting one instance of the associated character of picarooning at this time in the West Indies.

Among the pamphlets of the Harleian Miscellany will be found, under the title of " Proceedings of the Forces of their Majesties, King William and Queen Mary, in the Carribee Islands," a letter of Thomas Spencer, Secretary to the Honourable Sir Timothy Thornhill, being historical memoranda of the year 1689 and 1690. After noticing that before the war against France had been proclaimed, about the middle of September, 1689, a French privateer had landed at the Five Islands, near Antigua, and taken off several negroes; and that this armed vessel had met two English sloops, and taken one of them after some resistance; and that the other, making her escape, came in and gave an account of the action. Two vessels were manned from Barbadoes, with a company of Grenadiers of General Thornton's regiment, commanded by Captain Walter Hamilton, and these vessels took the French privateer the next day, with the prize sloop she had captured. It was stated, that in addition to thirty Frenchmen on board the privateer, were

2

found six Irishmen, who were tried by court-martial, and four executed. The narrative said, " deservedly executed," from some special circumstances, distinguishing four, while two were spared. In this freebooting war, the Du Cassé that had afterwards measured strength with Admiral Benbow, sailed with " bloody colours" at the mast. In the contests that ensued, forts were attacked, and towns burned, and men, women, and children taken prisoners. The prisoners were landed in the Islands nationally settled, each in his own, as a short riddance of an incumbrance; but invariably the negroes were reserved to be divided among the captors, and sold as marketable plunder. The spoils of the French Islands gave the English brandy and wine, in which they drank prosperity to Dutch William the King, and Mary the Consort Queen, in anticipation of the war that was proclaimed two years after, wnen the naval battle of La Hogue was fought and won.*

* As a specimen of the unexpected way in which men would be called upon to avow themselves as partizans, or the adherents of a cause in the unlooked for occurrences of the time, we may quote the following passage from Sir Hans Sloan's Journal, in his voyage from Jamaica to England. During his absence in Jamaica, the Revolution had displaced King James, and placed William and Mary on the throne. The first tidings of the change were received when within a few leagues of Plymouth, in the " Assistance" frigate, after the death of the Duke of Albemarle, whom he had accompanied to Jamaica as his physician. He reached England on the 29th of May, 1689. "I was sent," he relates, "in an armed boat, to get certain knowledge of the situation of public affairs, and to give a speedy account of it to the fleet, who were to stand off of that port till they were assured of their safety or danger. We had sight first of a boat

CHAPTER III.

FROM the treaty of peace, distinguished as the peace
of Ryswick, A.D. 1696, to that of Utrecht, A.D.
1713, an interval of seventeen years—in which the war
against France and Spain had been renewed, Gibraltar
taken, and the victories of Marlborough achieved—
hostilities were carried on in the West Indian Seas,
with all the barbarities inseparable from picarooning.
The Count de Choiseul Beaupré in 1707, as Governor
of St. Domingo, had re-instituted the Fraternity of
legalized Freebooters, known as Brethren of the Coast.
Sir Henry Morgan, twenty-five years before, under
treaties with Spain, had restrained the Buccaneers,
declaring, in his then capacity of Governor of Jamaica,
that hostile service against Spain, under any "foreign
power, state, or potentate," should be felony—punish-
able with death. But now the partizanship, under the
names of William and James, both recognized as Kings
of England, gave opportunities of pillage without
resort to any foreign prince, power, or potentate, and free
plundering prevailed in the Colonies. In Queen Anne's
reign the family animosities being renewed under the
cause of James—the first Pretender—a vessel of forty-
six (46) guns, called "La Revanche de la Reine
Anne"—Revenge on Queen Anne—was one of the

which was fishing some leagues from the land, whose master did
what he could to fly from us; but coming up with him, asking what
news, and where the King was, he asked—*what King we meant?* for
that King William was well at Whitehall, and King James in
France.

most successful marauders at sea. The House of
Hanover succeeded to the throne in the first year of
the peace of Utrecht. The Rebellion of 1715 being
quelled in Scotland, and Louis XIV. dead, King
George of Hanover decided on the year 1717 as a
befitting time, by proclamation,* to put an end to the
scourge of the Buccaneers.

* George Rex, having been informed that several subjects of Great
Britain have committed, since the 24th June, of the year 1705, divers
piracies and robberies in the seas of the West Indies, in the neigh-
bourhood of our plantations, which have caused very great losses to
the merchants of Great Britain, and others, merchants in those parts,
notwithstanding the orders which we have given to place on foot
forces sufficient to reduce these pirates. Nevertheless, to accomplish
this more efficaciously, we have found it fitting, by and with the
advice of our Privy Council, to publish this our Royal Proclamation,
promising and declaring by this present, that all and each of the
pirates who shall submit before the 5th of September, 1718, before
one of our Secretaries for Great Britain or Ireland, or before any
Governor, or Sub-Governors of any of our Colonies beyond the seas,
shall have our gracious pardon for the piracies which they may have
committed before the 5th of January next ensuing. We enjoin and
most expressly command all our admirals, captains, and other sea
officers, as well as our governors and commandants of our forts,
castles, or other places in our colonies, and all other officers, civil and
military, to seize all pirates who shall refuse, or neglect to submit
themselves conformably to this present. We declare further, that all
persons who may discover or arrest, or cause to be discovered and
arrested, one or more of these pirates, after the 6th of September,
1718, in such manner that they shall fall into the hands of justice, to
be punished according to their crimes, shall receive for recompense,
that is to say, for each commander of a ship, the sum of £100
sterling; for each lieutenant, master, quarter-master, carpenter,
and gunner, £40 sterling; for each sub-officer, £30; and for each
private £20. And if any soldier or sailor belonging to their troop
or ships, during the time above-mentioned, shall seize, or cause to be
seized, any one of these commanders, he shall have for each, £200

The proclamation made the seizing a runagate Freebooter as profitable an adventure as a dashing piracy.
It was much easier to shout on the dogs to the fray
than to whistle them off. The notorious freebooter,
Edward Teache, a native of Spanishtown, Jamaica, com-
monly known as "Blackbeard the pirate," was in La
Revanche de la Reine Anne, "under a French commission," turning his back on the proclamation and the
amnesty. He had captured the "Great Allen," a valuable English vessel; he had stripped her, and landed the
crew in the Island of St. Vincent, where he had burnt
his prize. A few days after he had fallen in with the
"Scarborough," a royal warship; after fighting her for
some hours he had beaten her off. The "Scarborough"
was short-handed, with a sick crew. Blackbeard, running through the Carribbean Sea, was everywhere successful, and everywhere dreaded. He had reached
Jamaica, had plundered and destroyed several merchant ships, and making off for Charleston to get what
he could coming out of that port. He was slain by
Captain Maynard in a hand-to-hand fight on the deck
of Captain Maynard's own vessel. Blackbeard's ship
was the Alabama of her day. His example in re-
jecting the amnesty, captivating the runagates, a wonderful excitement was active again, and piracy assumed
a character still bold but of comparatively small pretensions.

sterling; which sums shall be paid by the Lord Treasurer, or by the
commissioners of our treasury for the time being, upon being required by this present. Given at Hampton Court, the 5th of September, 1717, in the fourth year of our reign.

CHAPTER IV.

THOSE who have sailed through the blue waters of
the Bahamas, will recall the luxuriant aspect of the
Low Islands successively rising out of their shelves and
shoals. Their green appearance in the midst of chan-
nels delicately azure and bright, between island and
island renders them attractive, though their verdure
is little more than the vegetation of brushwood, and
their variety but sands and lagoons. This group,
anciently the Lucayos, composed of several hundred
islets and rocks and reefs, was tenanted when Columbus
discovered them, by a simple and happy people, remarkable for their gentleness. Only a few of them
have their surfaces diversified by rocks and ridges, or
rise into hilly undulations; not many have any elevation above the surrounding reefs. The outer ocean
becoming suddenly unfathomable beyond the barrier
walls of corals,—Columbus in sailing onward came
unexpectedly on the multitude of islands.*

* These islets, the first sample of the New World that greeted the
eyes of Columbus, are no where so vividly described as in the pages
of Washington Irving. "He landed on them on Friday the 12th of
October, 1492. As he approached the shore, Columbus, who was
disposed for all kinds of agreeable impressions, was delighted with
the purity and suavity of the atmosphere, the crystal transparency
of the sea, and the extraordinary beauty of the vegetation. He
beheld also fruits of an unknown kind, upon the trees which over-
hung the shores. On landing, he threw himself on his knees, kissed
the earth, and returned thanks to God with tears of joy. * * * *
The Spaniards remained all day on shore, refreshing themselves
after the anxious voyage amidst the beautiful groves of the island,
and returned on board. late in the evening delighted with all they

The situation of these Bahamas relatively with the Florida channel, and the Gulf stream, had given them an importance that rendered unaccountable the neglect with which they had been viewed, until the House of Lords addressed the King, some time after 1700, on the necessity of giving them a Governor and a Government. Up to this period the only consideration they had received was that of not being available for any European power, as long as the pirates nestled there. They could have—while that lawless occupancy continued—little maritime importance for national hostility. Harbour island was fortified. It defended the greater and loftier island of New Providence, where the Freebooters had a sort of excursion ground, in which they roamed at large, indulging the luxury of being

> "————free as nature first made man,
> When wild in woods the noble savage ran."

Andros Island, to the westward, was a shelter from the Florida channel. A space of clear water of no breadth, lengthened out like a canal between its borders and the shores of New Providence, with a chain of rocks and keys extending to Exuma, was called the

had seen." "On the evening of the 14th of October, the Admiral set off at day-break with the boats of the ships to reconnoitre the island, directing his course to the north-east. The coast was surrounded by a reef of rocks, within which there was depth of water and sufficient harbour to receive all the ships in Christendom. The entrance was very narrow; within there were several sand banks, but the water was still as in a pool." He was among the great cluster of the Lucayos or Bahama islands, stretching from the coast of Florida to Hisponiola, covering the northern coast of Cuba.—(*Life and Voyages of Columbus*, Vol. i., Book iv., chapter I.)

tongue of the ocean. It was difficult of access. Reefs and breakers hemmed its entrance. The Paradisaic Pandemonium within, in which the sea-rovers revelled when they changed from an ocean life to one on shore, was as unapproachable as Rasselas's happy valley. Though not freshened by rivulets and streams, the grassy slopes, composed of a close sward (the digitaria stolonifera), called Bahama grass, with occasional clumps of palms to adorn them, was varied by pools of water. The groves were rather shrubberies than wooded clusters,* but the hills had fertile glades, with herbs and fruits for refreshment. A range of rocky heights along the sea-board, had a ridge further inland called the Blue Hills. The intervening valley behind the heights and the ridge was a wilderness of cedar copices, with intricate pathways through them, and the flat country beyond was interrupted by ponds and morasses. The air was balmy, the verdure was perpetual, and the whole aspect pleasant. The climate was mild and delightful; not torrid in summer nor bleak in winter. Serene skies prevailed generally through the year, the northern blasts of the cold season not being of long continuance. The weather was often not cloudy, even when strong north winds were blowing. The mornings were cool, and the evenings soft and genial. The undulating scenery looked cultured, so pleasantly intermixed were trees and herbage without cultivation. Every thicket was a bower festooned with vines and flowers. Birds in abundance sought

* They abounded with a peculiar thorn, the *Catesbeia Spinosa*, with green pendulous blossoms.

the smooth lagoons, and flamingoes nestled in the sheltered cypress swamps in thousands. The sea breezes were constant, and the pleasant island might be said to be fanned by breezes unceasingly, but, being within the range of hurricanes, a day of storm was a day of havoc and destruction.*
The population was five hundred pirates. Their general rendezvous was Harbour Island. Under the free and confidential reciprocations that constituted the social code of the Buccaneer Brotherhood, the life of a

---

* European and tropical vegetables and fruits thrive together in the Bahamas, and are abundant; beef and mutton, and poultry are plentiful. The shores swarm with fish; and turtle are there enough to supply all Europe. Ambergris is occasionally found. Ship timber is produced in quantity for building as well as for planking vessels. Sponges of a good quality are washed on the islets. Shells are collected for cameos, and the water from the wells at New Providence has the desirable quality of keeping good at sea for any length of time.—(*Montgomery Martin's British Colonies.*)

To the genial weather of the islands may be contrasted a night scene under date of Sunday, September 4th, from Dana's vivid ocean pictures, in his "Two Years before the Mast." He describes the light breeze gradually dying away to a dead calm before midnight : the darkness black as Erebus, palpable and appalling—the talk on board low-toned and whispering:—the vessel lying motionless on the water :—the sails clewed up, and breast lines hauled in without any of the customary singing at the ropes. An electric light at the mast-head perceived as a ball of fire, and then presently descending as a star, and disappearing and re-appearing :—the falling drops of rain heavy and single; the random lightning coming on : the terrific flash with the sudden peal of thunder, right over head, and the rain suddenly pouring down like a falling ocean ; peal after peal ensuing, with the sea fitfully seen in a gleam of light. Not a breath of air stirring, darkness that might be felt continuing. At seven bells, the watch, that had turned in, comes on deck to find a fine clear sunny morning, with a good breeze and all sail set.

pirate ashore was all enjoyment. Conscious existence was instinctive happiness.

The dissolute coteries of Harbour Island were planning a thousand things consequent on Colonel Burnet's Bermudan proclamation inviting allegiance. It was a proclamation put forth in anticipation of the King's amnesty, announced soon after by Captain Woodes Rodgers when he arrived in the Bahamas with the authorized document declaring a general pardon and oblivion of all past pillage and piracy. The fort on Harbour Island was taken possession of on the 27th of July, 1718, and in the presence of three hundred inhabitants gathered together there, the proclamation was read that made sure the liberty they were enjoying, with the possession of the Eden they occupied. Captain Rodgers found no hesitation with them in accepting the terms he offered—tranquil obedience, submission to his authority as their Governor, in the name of George of Hanover, King of England.

CHAPTER V.

" When spite of conscience pleasure is pursued,
Man's nature is unnaturally pleas'd."

Young's Night Thoughts.

WHAT is unnatural is painful. It never fails to disgust eventually, however eagerly the unnatural pleasure may be sought after. Whether it was satiety of debauchery, or whether it was awaking thought when " pain of mind surpasses pain of sense," that led the Freebooters to yield to the amnesty—they took gladly the oath of allegiance, and with it their certificates of surrender, and settled down into domestic life. Revellings had been only opiates for inquietude within—

> " ————————turbid streams
> Of rapturous exultation, which swell high
> Like land-floods that impetuous pour awhile,
> To sink at once and leave us in the mire."

When we consider that a mere animal has no such appetites as a vicious man, that the ravening of the one is simply the body's necessity, while the hunger of the other includes in it the satisfying both soul and body, character must shape the design and aim of gratification. The appetites of sin are unnatural. Toils oppress the body. Dissipation and excess, feasts, and intemperance, licentiousness of life, are drudgeries. The sensuous desires of a craving spirit obtain their gratification under exhaustion. Whatever those appetites may . be, they are unnatural; body and soul cannot find their repose together. The rest that should restore the one, wastes in torture of thought the other. They have a natural relation only when both together find satisfaction in tranquillity. Reasonably gratified, they do not go beyond moderation. In uneasiness under the soul's hunger, a sin-indulging body rushes into shiftings and devices, and plans and exploits ; stability or calmness is not a possible condition. There is no contentment. Weariness is not soothed by solitude; fatigue is not refreshed by the slumber of repose. The heart withers, the spirit languishes. The desire is inordinate, and out of nature it seeks gratification only to be tormented by reflection.

Pardon and peace were felt to be natural wants: the amnesty gave both. The opportunity of lawlessness, when submission was claimed by no authority, had made the sea-rovers pirates. The recognition of a master, upheld by obedience and law, was to transform them into citizens. The community of Freebooters settled as farmers; but when war stirred again the business-world into an unquiet activity, a new energy was given to the settlers now known as the Bahama islanders. The prizes taken from legitimate enemies, brought in and condemned in their port, supplied them with legitimate trade. Navigators in the pursuit of commerce threaded the labyrinth of rocks and shelves, now safe as passages to the Carribbean Sea. The daring and adventurous spirit of the islanders made them useful as aids to those who needed help in difficulties. Their mariners found employment, and derived profit from the salvage for ships saved under peril, and from the cargoes rescued when the vessel was lost. The school of enterprise in which they had been brought up prepared them to be beneficial occupants of those islands in times of danger and distress.

The Government of the Bahamas was resumed by the Crown, when Captain Woodes Rodgers renewed in the Island of Providence the settlement which had been attempted there in the reign of Charles the

Secon1, but soon after abandoned. Though reduced in population, the island soon became the resort of hundreds of adventurers, satisfied with what was to be done lawfully. The colony of *Rogues* was broken up. The hundred soldiers that accompanied Captain Rodgers made a magnificent garrison, with the five hundred men already there all armed. Six persons, brought purposely, were sworn in a council for legislative and administrative business. There was immediately an organized and defensive garrison. The want felt being active occupation, in a community with whom occupation had been enterprise, a watch and ward marine was projected, and seamen readily volunteered to man a vigilance fleet to visit the numerous Cays scattered about, every one of which was a harbour for suspected craft.

Among the confidential mariners engaged in this service was one Vane, a buccaneer of the sworn brotherhood. He had come into the Bahamas with silver stolen from Spaniards, who had recently fished up treasure from a galleon that had foundered in the Gulf of Florida. He had robbed them while wrecking. Vane was pursy, and he was influential at the rendezvous in Providence when Governor Rodgers arrived with his three men-of-war ships and proclaimed King George's government and King George's amnesty.

The proclamation of pardon to the pirates had been conceived in the spirit of the maxim—*injuriarum remedium est oblivio*. In every treaty of peace during the years the outrageous system of harassing an enemy by buccaneering had been legalized, provision was made for submission on all sides to the flagitious acts committed. In announcing oblivion of the past, it was declared that every one who had been licensed had been legally commissioned to do what he had done, and each was to keep what he had acquired. Many of the adventurers who had surrendered, it was to be presumed, would yet think it was hardly worth while to accept as grace pardon for deeds that war would make lawful violence. They bided their time.

CHAPTER VI.

TRIAL strengthens the soul either for good or evil. There are depths in Satan through which a man sinks to touch ground, not to rest, but to rise again to the surface and " to roll darkling down the torrent to his fate."

Vane had predetermined to be on the water once more, and, in spite of the amnesty, to set up again as a freebooter. He had entered as a volunteer, and was commissioned as captain on board one of the armed ships. Captain Rodgers was providing for scouring the islands. Just in proportion as the proclamation excited security among those navigating the Bahamas, a rogue who would run the gauntlet would be extraordinarily successful. Vane had with him one Rackam among the volunteers in his vessel. They counted themselves fifty in force. Vane proposed to these fifty to start off with the vessel they were on board of. What he proposed the fifty acceded to. Sending a fire ship into the anchorage of the king's men-of-war, the Rose, the Milford and her mate ; the Milford, in her effort to move out of the way, got aground—the Rose barely towing out of danger. Vane escaped. This host of pledged adherents to the House of Hanover, who had sworn fidelity in an oath that acquainted them with a disputed succession, considered their fealty no better for the House of Brunswick than for the family of Stuart. They were on the sea again hurraing for the Fraternity of Freebooters. The proclamation of pardon was intelligible enough, but the oath of allegiance had made out there was "no king in Israel ;" and as they could do "what seemed right in their own eyes," they set up trade for themselves, their hearts echoing—

" For pleas of right, let statesmen vex their head,
    Battle's my business, and my guerdon bread;
    And with the sworded Switzer, I can say,
    The best of causes is the best of pay."

Among the comrades and consorts associated with Vane, sailing in "Independence," we have mentioned Rackam. He held the appointment of quarter-master—a grade only inferior to that of captain. He was the second in command. The freebooters at this time could now assume no national license. Any flag was an enemy, and any ship a prize. Vane with his vessel and companions, clear of the Bahamas, ran in sight of a French man-of-war. His ship's company were for fighting the Frenchman as they crossed him between Cuba and St. Domingo, that is, between Cape

Maize and Cape Nicholas Mole. A council from on
board the associated ships was held in the usual way
of taking opinions with the Fraternity of Freebooters,
and Vane refusing to fight, was voted unworthy of
his command. He was put adrift in one of the
consorts at their disposal, and sent to shift how he
could elsewhere, and Rackam was made commander in
his stead.*

* Vane was put adrift with all those who voted with him against
fighting the French ship of war. With a person named Robert Deal,
the crew amounted to sixteen (16) altogether. Vane and these men
were furnished, by Rackam, with a small shallop, which had been
taken the day before with provisions, and ammunition enough for
a cruise. They sailed to the Bay of Honduras, and took there a
sloop and two piriaguas. Deal was made master of the captured
sloop. On the 16th of December, 1718, they hoisted the black flag.
In February a tornado cast them ashore on a small desert island.
The ship of one Holford, an old buccaneer, coming into this island,
Vane besought him to take him off; but Holford knowing him to be
habitually treacherous, let him know that as he was out of the
amnesty, he would betray him to justice. When Holford soug..t
him, he found him gone; but happening to be dining on board a
trading vessel soon afterwards, on the Indian coast, he discovered
Vane in the hold of the ship, employed as one of the crew, taken on
board in compassion as a cast away sailor. Holford sent his mate
for him, who took him, menacing him pistol in hand. He was delivered over to the Admiralty in Jamaica, under the reward for a
runagate, and was convicted and executed. Robert Deal, in the
consort sloop, had been previously taken and hung. Vane's fate
showed there was no friendship among villains. The success that
had made him formidable made him a valuable subject for betrayal.
Though found peaceful, yet known to have been a pirate, and assured
that his breaking away after surrender would aggravate his crime, he
dared not to plead his pardon. He suffered death in 1719, as an irre-
claimable pirate.

CHAPTER VII.

THE marvellous commands admiration. In the
heathen mythology the demigod, wonderful by being
more than human, is an alluring object. The interest
of the marvellous is always effective. In an age in
which giants and magicians were the great actors in
fiction, and fairies divided attention with the heroes of
romance, the wonderful was indispensable in what
happened. Though the agency in the things of our
time be the natural, and not the supernatural, the
marvellous in life, in manners, in character, and in
situation, is still requisite to command popular favour.
The men and women, energetic and ardent, have
morality enough for the public appetite, if they can
be sensible of neglect, susceptible of passion, and can
give a warrant for their love or their hatred, their
clemency or revenge, in some sort of sentiment, under
actions regulated by no ordinary rule. These remarks
introduce to our notice Rackam, the contemporary of
Blackbeard, sailing with two very remarkable associates. Rackam leaves a name in Jamaica more
memorable than that of any of the Picaroons.

On the 24th November, 1718, Rackam, in command
of an armed brigantine, had in his company of pirates
the two remarkable mariners we have mentioned. They
were noticeable ship-mates—plump, active, and prompt,
and very resolute. From Jamaica he had cruised up
to Bermuda, taking prizes wherever he went, whether
North or South, East or West. The outer solitary

3

islets of the Bahamas were visited as careening places. There he refitted his vessel and rid himself of his captures. On learning that Governor Rodgers had heard of his whereabout, he started off and left the Bahama islets altogether. Two years had passed in scape-grace adventures, when Rackam came into these waters again, and sought the Cays of Cuba, there to establish a household. He gathered together in concealment a little colony, and eat and drank, and merrily feasted till money and provisions were expended, when he went to sea again.

A Spanish guarda-costa coming with a contraband prize into the channel where his vessel lay, Rackam found his place no longer secret. He promptly prepared to take his leave and depart, but not without carrying away something worth the danger he had run by being known. He seized, silently in the night, the contraband prize of the Spaniard, a well loaded vessel, and left in its place his own crazy brigantine as an exchange. It was now August, 1720, and he was between the islets that string the south coast of Cuba, and the northern waters of Jamaica. He wanted men. The proclamation had thinned the company of freebooters. He determined to enter the harbours of the English colony, and overhaul the small craft, and recruit his strength by volunteers from the coasters. In the beginning of September he was in Green Island harbour, stealing nets and tackling from fishing boats. He landed in St. Domingo, where two old French buccaneers were hunting wild hogs at sundown; these he got to join him as an addition to

his crew. In the latter ten days of October his vessel
had successively scoured the whole north side of
Jamaica. He had entered Dry Harbour. Getting
possession there of a sloop with its lading, he was led
into reckless confidence on finding that men who had
deserted their boat at the sight of his pirate vessel, had
returned in a short time and besought him to receive
them among his crew as comrades.

Intelligence of Rackam's doings, while coasting
Jamaica, had been communicated from a canoe at
Ocho-rios,* and transmitted to the governor, Sir
Nicholas Laws, a. wealthy and enterprising planter,
then acting as interim governor, waiting the arrival of
the son of Dutch Bentinck, Duke of Portland, coming
out as captain-general of the colony. Sir Nicholas Laws
was a man of great decision and energy. He fitted
out immediately an armed sloop in quest of the freebooter, or whatever else it might prove to be. The
despatched vessel was committed to Captain Barnet,
and was manned with a number of hands. Sir Nicholas
had already manifested great promptitude in matters
connected with plundering the sea-side plantations,
stealing away negroes—the exploits of Picaroons and
known to be commissioned by Spanish authorities. In his official quality he had sent to Cuba and
demanded restitution of slaves, stolen, or carried away
since the peace. He had signalized two pillagers by
their names as Brown and Wynter,† well known as

* The Spaniards called it Chorreras—the Falls.
† The short war with Spain had sent a multitude of sailors wan-
dering about the country in search of employment. Brown and

commissioned marauders sailing out of Cuba. At this time, Benito Alphonzo del Monzano, the governor, had used the plea of Christian conversion as rendering slaves free men. As they had become Catholic Chris-

Wynter, the notorious pirates, had now fitted out several vessels at Trinidad de Cuba, for the purpose of capturing the negroes on the seaside plantations. The parish of St. Ann suffered severely. It was the richest of the north side parishes, and being subject to frequent attacks, was armed for resistance. " A domestic tragedy," says Bridges in his *Annals of Jamaica*, "was acted there, scarcely equalled in the sanguinary annals of those times. The proprietor of a considerable settlement, who had repeatedly repelled these lawless plunderers, one night, in the security of his success, and in the bosom of his family, was boasting that they would never venture to attack him more. The picaroons had stolen across from Cuba, and were at the moment lying concealed in the brushwood round the house, waiting till the family had retired to rest. With savage inhumanity they listened to the domestic effusions of presumed security ; they measured the provocation and determined on revenge. When all was quiet within, they barricaded the house from without, and applied fire to it in all directions. They heard, unmoved, the agonizing cries of the helpless parents and their dying children ; and in the morning nothing remained but the smoking ruins of the house, and the ashes of sixteen human beings. Deeds of atrocity, scarce less appalling, were of frequent occurrence on the north side of the island, and a sloop of war was therefore fitted out, by subscription, for its protection. These repeated acts of hostility were but feebly resented by the detention of such Spanish effects as were found in Jamaica ; but to provide against a recurrence of them, a disposable force was raised by a capitation levy ; and one man for every hundred negroes was enrolled, accoutred, and trained. Thus an effective body of seven hundred men was maintained, and distributed along the coast, without inconvenience to themselves, or expense to the island." Bridges' *Annals of Jamaica*, Vol. i., chapter ix., page 348, 350. In this protective measure originated what was known as " the Deficiency Law," in which a fine was paid by plantations for any *deficiency* in these relative numbers.

tians, they were no longer slaves but fugitives, and amenable alone to law for crimes they may commit. They were, he asserted, free subjects. As to the vessels, he said, they had been seized as smugglers, and were properly confiscated. Sir Nicholas Laws, in his reply to the governor, denounced the vessels committing these outrages as pirates. He stigmatized the governor of the district of Trinidad, who had, in this communication, made religion a pretext for protecting scoundrels, as being himself no better than a pirate ; warning him that men who were sheltered by such a plea should suffer the penalty of piracy.

Rackam having made his appearance on the coast just after this correspondence, he was sought after as one of the licensed pillagers protected and accredited by the Spanish Government, and whom he desired to seize to make examples of. His capture, with his two remarkable associates, characterized in the history of their lives by incidents more like fables than realities, is an instance that "Truth is strange, stranger than fiction."

CHAPTER VIII.

RACKAM, before he possessed himself of the prize taken away from the Spanish man-of-war, among the Cays of Cuba, called the Queen's Gardens, had performed some memorable exploits. We shall advert only to what he had done between Jamaica and St. Domingo, immediately after he had been put in command of Vane's brigantine. The change of vessel effected by abandoning his brigantine for his Spanish contraband prize, kept him from recognition as the pirate that had taken a ship from Madeira. He had detained and pillaged her, and then given her back to the master, after "making his market out of her," putting on board of her one Hosea Tiddel, a Jamaica tavern keeper, whom he had taken from another prize, permitting him in this way to regain his Jamaica home. He had very inconveniently boarded and possessed himself of a ship laden with convicts from Newgate bound for the plantations, and was glad when the prize was re-taken by a war cruiser. There would never be a want of desperate adventurers to set up as pirates in these seas, when the clearings of the prisons were made a source for supplying settlers to the Colonies. On the coast of Jamaica he was "running at low game," as it was called, but his necessity, the want of hands, obliging him to increase his company, he sought for volunteers out of coasters in the plantations. In this way he had an accession to his crew in Dry Harbour.

Rackam, just arrived in Negril Bay, was drinking on board with the crew of a fishing boat distinguished by an Indian name then common as a *piragua*.*

> "There's wealth and ease for gentlemen,
> And simple folk might fight and fen,
> But here we are all of one accord,
> For ilka man that's drunk is a Lord."

He had prevailed on the piragua people to come and

* Piragua, a fishing boat, is an Indian word derived from *pira*

partake of a bowl of punch, with which he was then regaling his men, and to smoke their pipes with him, at the moment when Captain Barnet, rounding Negril point, had come upon him. The number of the men that had then adventitiously joined Rackam were nine. They were all armed with muskets and cutlasses. He hastily weighed anchor with his visitors. He was under weigh hurrying to get away from the search vessel with a light breeze blowing off the land, when Barnet gave him chase, and out-sailing him, took him a prize, and brought him into Port Royal on the 16th November, 1720. Captain Rackam and eight men, specified as his crew, were tried at an Admiralty assize, convicted and executed a fortnight after their capture, Rackam and two of his men being hung in chains. At an adjourned court in January following, the remainder of the prisoners were tried. The nine who had gone on board as visitors from the piragua, were charged not with piracy, no such act was provable against them, but with joining Rackam with a piratical intention. For this constructive offence they were

a fish. It occurs in the name of many fishes of the continent, as *piracuta* in the Essequibo : pira-poca, the gar-fish : and the famous *pira-roucou*, the red-fish of the Demerara, the Sudis gigas. The piratees, the people of the Pedro plains of Jamaica, are descendants of Indian fishermen, the only remnant of the aboriginal race of the island remaining, though of mixed blood. Pirates, were the navigators of piraguas, fishing boats, the first vessel used in piracy in the West Indian seas. The pirata, or pirate of the Mediterranean, derived his name from a Greek word πειραω to attempt an enterprise in a way representing the predatory character of the Corsair. The Indian pirata was only a bold pillager, plundering from the piragoa, when the navigators of the piragua, took to piracy.

tried, and being convicted, were hanged also. They were probably picaroon adventurers, concerned in independent pillage, that common class of Freebooters, whom Sir Nicholas Laws had referred to in his demand for Brown and Wynter, from the Governor of Cuba. The barricaded house in St. Ann's, in which a whole family fastened in were burned alive, being, two years after, a fearful instance of the characteristic marauding of these piragua pillagers.

Beside the Frenchmen, whom Rackam had taken on board in St. Domingo, two of whom having witnessed his acts of piracy, were made Admiralty evidences, there were two others to whom the clemency of respite and eventual reprieve was extended; these were Bonney and Read. When about to be sentenced after trial, they announced themselves to be women, and to be then with child.

Anne Bonney was the daughter of an Irish attorney-at-law, who had deserted a wife and family in the City of Cork, and had betaken himself to America with the servant girl, by whom he had this child Anne, before his departure. He had fixed himself in Carolina, forsaking law for merchandise. Having made a fortune, he had settled as a planter. Anne's mother had died, and she had been remembered, in charge of her father's house, a comely girl, reputed to have a fortune in expectancy. She had been addressed by young men of good family in Carolina, but had turned from all to marry a sailor, a dashing young adventurer with no means but his luck. Her father had banished her from his house, and the skipper, with his young wife, thrown entirely on the world, had found his way to New Providence, the then resort of all the refractory spirits of the time. The colonists had shipped off in irons their Governor Elias Hacket, some few summers before, and were then revelling in the islands, the masters of themselves, with all creation for pillage and piracy. Anne Bonney having little steadiness for such society, had eloped with Captain Rackam in man's clothes. She had been living some time in secrecy in one of the outer islands, nursing her first child, when she betook herself definitively with Rackam to sea, in the character of one of his crew. In this disguise, she was his companion in Negril Bay. In all his piratical exploits she had displayed courage and intrepidity. She had distinguished herself among her shipmates, by showing a spirit of resistance when all but one companion had yeilded at the boarding of the vessel off Negril. This other resolute sailor was unknown to any but Anne Bonney, and her captain. Rackam seeing what seemed to him suspicious familiarity between Bonney and Read, had shown himself jealous of the intimacy, and had threatened Bonney with violence for it, when she disclosed the history of the remarkable person, whose familiar acquaintance he had noticed.

Mary Read had achieved more than ordinary distinction in the pirate service. To courage and daring she had united such skill as a swordsman, that she was foremost in all desperate adventures. Becoming a special favourite with Anne Bonney, her regard and admiration had ripened into affection, for the supposed seaman. In the plenitude of passion, she had avowed her love

for him, when Read disclosed her sex, and surprised
her with the discovery that she was a woman like herself, whom a spirit of enterprise had carried to sea,
after she had been serving as a trooper in Marlborough's wars in Flanders.

The story of Mary Read's life has more romance in
it than ordinary. Her mother, an Englishwoman, had
married a sailor, like many sea-faring persons of the
time of a family in good circumstances. She was very
young, when she became a wife, and her husband
going a voyage never returned. She gave birth to a
son, while he was absent; and too young to be unsus-
ceptible of passion, or uncorrupted by intrigue, on
becoming again pregnant, under a sense of discredit
to her husband's family, she betook herself into the
country away from them, and there gave birth to a
girl child. After some two or three years of estrange-
ment from her connexions, the boy child died, and
then she hit upon the expedient of passing the surviving
child Mary, on her husband's mother, as the boy she
was known to have given birth to, and taken with her
into the country. The mother of her husband, as con-
solation for her sailor son, gladly received the daughter-
in-law, and the supposed grandson. As the mother
refused to be separated from the child, the grandmother settled upon it an allowance of a crown a week
for support, and the widowed mother lived apart
from her husband's kindred.

The daughter Mary thus reared passed as a boy.
Concealment continued to effect what she sought in the
weekly payment of the allowance, till the grandmother

died, when the maintenance ceased. The disguised youth, having attained a serviceable age, was hired to a French lady as a foot-boy. In her French service she was brought into acquaintance with continental life. Feeling an ardour for adventure the foot-boy's employment was abandoned for the sea. Self-reliant, rather than volatile, and an adept at an assumed character, she quitted the sea service, and joined a regiment of infantry, entering as a cadet for the wars in Flanders. Finding a commission not easily attainable, she changed from the infantry to the cavalry. The wars under Marlborough found her behaving valiantly. One of her comrades, a young Fleming of remarkable beauty, won her womanly heart in her disguise. The strangeness of her behaviour under the excitement of love, attracted attention, and she was supposed to be mad, till the discovery of her sex by her companion of the same tent. It had been so managed as not to appear intentional on Read's part. She made it only to the object of her affection, and disclosed it as an explanation of the mystery of her behaviour. She made no concession to him, though she loved him ardently, but as his lawful wife. Their mutual attachment being avowed, and the romance of her concealed sex disclosed, their marriage was publicly celebrated by the regiment. Liberal contributions were made to set up the couple in a hostelry called the "Three Horse Shoes." The strange history of the wedded pair drew a world of patronage. Business, however, was not attractive enough, when the early death of the husband left Mary a young widow. She betook herself in her former

disguise to the army again. She was a soldier in the
frontier wars, and fought at the battles of Ramilles,
Oudenarde, and Malplaquet, till the peace of Utrecht
sent her adrift on the world.

From a discharged soldier, she entered as a sailor
on board a Dutch vessel bound for the West Indies, and
fell into the hands of pirates. Being English she was
received among the "Brethren of the Coast," and was
associated with the Fraternity when she united her fortune with Anne Bonney and Captain Rackam. *

CHAPTER IX.

THE act of mutiny perpetrated by Vane and Rackam
had thrown Mary Read among avowed pirates again.
When taken prisoner on board the Dutch ship sailing
in her disguise, she was submitting to the chances of
a seaman's fate. Experience had reconciled her to
a lawless life. Conscience was asleep. Its reproofs
made no part of her thoughts and apprehensions.

* The treaty concluded in Madrid, 13th June, 1731, subsidiary to
the treaty of Utrecht, in its fourth article stipulated for the "restoration of all goods and effects of the subjects of Spain, which could be
proved to have been seized and confiscated in the dominions of His
Britannic Majesty in the war past." The subjection of the Bahamas
to British rule at the time of this treaty must have made the amnesty,
at least in the apprehension of those who had availed themselves of
it, and who remained where their pillage had been stowed, so little
an exemption from inquiry that they must have felt their possessions
insecure.

Captain Rackam, before he became acquainted with her assumed character, observing her to be, though desperate, gentle hearted and generous, sought to learn the sentiments which had influenced so noticeable a person to take to a Buccaneer life. " Why," he asked one day when she drew his special attention, " why do I see you following a vocation that seems not congenial with your character, knowing that it has the certainty of a felon's death as a penalty?" " As for that," replied the woman sailor, " I hold it no reason for abandoning a life of adventure. All those who throw themselves into the service are brave. If it were not for the penalty of death, pirates would be all poltroons. Courageous men would starve ashore. To my choice the penalty should not be less than death. It is *that* fear of a felon's death that keeps dastardly men out of the service. Those ashore who cheat widows and rob orphans, and are just bold enough to oppress their neighbours, because they are too poor to seek justice, would be robbing at sea. A crowd of rogues would be plundering, if pillage had no dangers. Merchants would be deterred from venturing a valuable cargo afloat. Freebooting would be a trade not worth following. The rewards of piracy are only for the brave." She manifested that " desperation of will that tramples fear, and makes it as though it were not." Dr. Bushnell, in his exquisite work the *New Life*, says in this desperation of will, " human nature shows its dignity from its ruins."

Artisans on board captured vessels were an acquisition. If they were found willing for the Corsair service they were retained. A handsome young artisan had been taken in one of the prizes. Being reconciled to be among his captors, he was regularly enrolled a Freebooter. From friendship with him as a companion, Mary Read found herself trammelled in love with him. Pleasure in conversation, grew into passionate delight socially. A brawl had ended in a challenge to the carpenter to fight a duel. The disguised woman sailor had witnessed the challenge, and impatient to rescue her favourite's life now exposed to danger, where challenges were terminated with death to one of the combatants, Mary Read rose and perpetrating some unbearable insult on the brawling shipmate, she required that he should efface the *last* insult before he ventured to avenge the *first*. Her trooper life had made her an expert swordsman. Relying on the mastery of her skill she fought her man, and running him through laid him dead at her feet. Her affection was prudent, her ardour was discreet. Love with her was not lust: the man for whom she felt her bosom burning must be saved; her hasty insult was her device for accomplishing his safety. When she disclosed her sex to the friend she had rescued, and avowed her attachment to him, she pledged her faith to him solemnly; and secretly became his wife. In a service in which there was no priest, no disclosure of the marriage occurred. She continued her disguise. The relations in which she and the carpenter, her friend, stood to each other were unknown to the world, till her imprisonment and trial.

Anne Bonney and Mary Read were reckoned the most intrepid of the pirate crew. Both were courageous, with no betrayal of feminine weakness. In

Mary Read more than in Anne Bonney, however, the heart intimated a loftier sentiment. She was high-minded ; scrupulous in principle. Both had formed irregular attachments, but Mary Read never faltered in steadfast faith. After her trial, when she told the history of her life, she asserted that she had never held womanly commerce with any but her lawful husbands, the deceased comrade of Flanders, and the carpenter friend she had attached herself to in the vessel in which she was captured, and none of her shipmates could say she ever had. Rackam had been permitted to see Anne Bonney, when led out to execution. She suppressed all emotion ; withheld all condolence. Without upbraid-ing him for her deviation from the path of duty as a wife, she ventured to tell him that failure in courage, made him the culprit he then stood. Feeling what desperate boldness had done for safety on a pirate's deck, she rebukingly said to him in parting from him for death, " had he fought as a man before he was taken, he would not be led away now to be hanged like a dog."

Mary Read died in her cell reprieved ; but Anne Bonney, who had been known to several Jamaica planters, when a virtuous and well reputed girl in her father's house in Carolina, was interceded for to be restored to her family. All the account left of her only states that she escaped a felon's fate, obtaining mercy when justice, satiated with its victims, could show forbearance.

John Rackam, with two associates, George Feather-stone and Richard Corner, were hung in chains in the islet called Rackam Cay, gibbeted as a terror to pirates. The hurricane two years after on the 28th of August, 1722, swept away the gibbet, the memorial of their fate. A letter of the time written by Mr. Atkins, the purser of His Majesty's ship Weymouth, one of the few vessels that rode out that "*great storm*," has this record. "Of fifty sail in Port Royal Harbour on that day, only four men of war, and two merchant ships, rode it out, but with all their masts and booms blown away. All the men we left at Gun Cay (coopering) were washed off and perished, except an *Indian* that drove into harbour on a *broken gallows* that had been there erected." This is not the last trace of Rackam; his name is perpetuated in the Rackam Cay, of Navigators' Charts to point out the channel into Port Royal.

SEQUEL

TO

One Hundred and Fifty Years Ago.

UNDER the title of One Hundred and Fifty Years Ago, we have exhibited the kind of piracy that succeeded licensed buccaneering in the West Indian Seas, and related some of the incidents of the time, in the career of Rackam, and his two women sailors. While the British suppressed picarooning by the proclamation of 1718, the Spanish Government carried on in undiminished vigour pillage by guarda-costas. In the year of the proclamation we have quoted in full, King George had quarrelled with Spain. War ensued, but ended very shortly. The Spanish fleet had been destroyed at Syracuse, and a pacification was effected, but upon so debateable a footing with reference to commerce in the West Indian Seas, that trading was not carried on without running all the risks of the Buccaneer period. Spain had her own way. If a vessel visited her colonies it was seized as contraband. If it only approached her coasts it was boarded and plundered. The peace of Utrecht was an event of 1713, that of Aix-la-chapelle of 1748. The interval had been one of little wars and great wars. Russia in 1721, from a Dukedom had

4

become an empire. Keuli-Khan in 1722, had usurped the Persian throne, and enriched himself out of the spoils of the Great Mogul with a clear two hundred and thirty-two millions of pounds sterling: the battles of Dettingen and Fontenoy had been fought :—a convention between Spain and Great Britain had, previous to a quarrel with France, been entered into, under the signature of Don Sabastian de la Quadra, setting forth that £68,000 pounds should be paid as value for ships seized in the West Indies by guarda-costas, irrespective of some other unascertained demands, to be decided by plenipotentiaries within the current A.D., 1739, when the convention should be ratified.

The spoliations of Spain, when all private adventuring had been put down, were sustained under very specific pretentions. Don Sabastian de la Quadra in a communication in anwer to memorials relative to vessels plundered, and to barbarities perpetrated, had said, addressing Sir Benjamin Keene, the British Minister at Madrid, "His Majesty the King of Spain commands me to tell you, Sir, that the treaty of 1667," (the treaty of 1670 was meant, which gave Jamaica to England in perpetual Sovereignty)—"does not contain in any of its articles, unless it be the eighth, any clause applicable to the navigation and commerce of the Indies ; the English have been wrong in supposing that the subjects of His Britannic Majesty have a right to sail to and trade in the West Indies ; they had only permission to sail to their own islands and plantations ; they are, therefore, *subject to confiscation*, if it appear that they had, *without necessity, made* the Spanish coasts."

The Treaty of 1670* detailed in a brief summary contains these covenants.

All hostilities should cease between the two Kings of Spain and England and their subjects ; and on both sides all commissions, letters of marque, &c., were to be called in, and declared null and void.

Prisoners on both sides detained by reason of acts of hostility hitherto committed in America were to be set at liberty.

Offences, injuries, and losses, suffered by either party in America were to be wholly buried in oblivion.

The King of Great Britain, his heirs and successors, were expressly declared to possess in full sovereignty and property, all countries, islands, colonies, &c., lying and situated in the West Indies, or in any part of America, which he or his subjects then held or possessed, insomuch that they neither can nor ought hereafter to be contested under any pretence whatever.

The subjects, merchants, captains, masters, and mariners of each ally respectively shall forbear and abstain from sailing to or trafficking in the ports and havens that have fortifications or magazines, and in all other places possessed by either party in the West Indies.

And finally, it was declared to be always understood that the freedom of navigation ought by no means to be interrupted, when there is nothing committed contrary to the true sense and meaning of the articles of the convention.

* Known as Sir William Godolphin's Treaty.

Notwithstanding that the convention, dated the 14th of January, 1739, specified that the interests of Spain and England in respect of their commerce should be adjusted and regulated for reciprocal reparation of damages sustained, and that the interests of the two crowns in regard to pretensions to trade and navigation in America and Europe should be settled, according to previous treaties, commencing with that of 1667 and ending with that of 1728, a declaration of war was issued on the 19th of October following, without waiting the final conference, which it was stipulated should take place within eight months.

The commissary's list of ships attacked, taken, or plundered by the Spaniards in the West Indian Seas within a period of ten years, from '28 to '38, amounted to fifty-two, with losses computed at £340,000; the £95,000 to be settled by Spain being represented as a balance of reparation on the reciprocal damages sustained which was to be remitted in four months.

CHAPTER XI.

THE movement to restrain Spain in her aggressive acts in the Carribbean Sea exhibited unaccountable vacillation and feebleness of purpose. Admiral Hosier had been sent, in 1726, with a strong fleet to blockade the Galleons, at that time the periodic plate ships, from the mining ports of South America. But his orders were only to make seizures of them when they were at sea, and then specifically as payment for the pillage committed by known guarda-costas or known vessels. The scheme of doing something in appearance and doing nothing in fact, was a deplorable exhibition of Sir Robert Walpole's temporizing views of national justice. Hosier anchored off the Bastimentos, appearing warlike without going to war. He remained there effecting no other change of place than a cruize before Carthagena. His vessels rotted and his men perished. Under his anomalous orders he was the ridicule of the enemy, and died at his station broken-hearted.

The Spanish Government put forth allegations that the guarda-costas made their seizures only when attempts were made at contraband trade. Having disallowed all traffic from sea with her colonies, Great Britain, in not restraining trade that Spain had prohibited, abetted the insolent conduct of her subjects. The King of Spain was defrauded in his own dominions; his reprisals were not aggressions, but his remedy for grievances. This justification will be found set forth in the Marquis de la Paz's letter to Mr. Stanhope, dated St. Ildefonso, September 30th, 1726. Noticing the squadrons then on the coasts of the Indies—a comprehensive word for all the central and southern American colonies, together with all the Antilles—he says :—" The complaint which has for its subject the conduct of the guarda-costas, and which censures their operations as infractions of commerce and of treaties, is most unjust in form and substance." " Those ships," he declared, " had done nothing at variance with the discharge of their coasting duties. They only hindered, with all available power, the unlawful and clandestine commerce carried on by nations in the West Indies. That commerce was solemnly prohibited by repeated treaties. Infringements of those treaties had been hitherto made, to the prejudice of his Spanish Majesty. Frauds were insolently perpetrated in his rightful dominions. On the part of his Britannic Majesty no restrictions had been applied to the misconduct of his subjects, acting in concert with other powers, in those parts of the Spanish dominions."

The instances of alleged aggressions were that vessels sailing to Jamaica were boarded off Cuba. They were taken into Cuban ports, and the crews turned adrift in open boats. Demands were made for these specified vessels detained and condemned, but the demands were answered insolently by Spanish governors. The propriety of those demands was manifested in the case of the galliot Anne, taken in July, 1728, by a guarda-costa, and carried into St. Jago de Cuba. The Duke of Newcastle had obtained an order for the restitution of this ship and cargo, and in default compensation was to be made in £10,000.

Other applications to the Spanish Government were made for reparation under similar spoliations, all very specifically enumerated. The indiscriminate character of the acts complained of, the flagitious nature of them, was signally shown in the Puerto-Rico guarda-costa brought into Jamaica by his Majesty's ship Launceston. This assumed guarda-costa was commanded by one

Matthew Luke, who called himself an Italian, and had boarded the Launceston, mistaking the ship for a merchant trader. He was a picaroon, known to have previously taken four English ships, and to have cut the throats of all their crews. Accredited as in command of a coastguard bark his pursuit was plunder. Matthew Luke and seven of his men suffered death as pirates at Port Royal, one man boasting at his trial that twenty Englishmen had been murdered by *his* hand alone.

In 1728 Hosier died. In 1739 the £95,000 which Spain had stipulated should be paid under the Convention of January of that year, had not been received, and Walpole, convinced that no compromise could be made, and that the option left him was either war or retirement from office, demanded, on this non-fulfilment of a fixed engagement, a renunciation by Spain of all right of search in West Indian Seas. This right had been the pretext for depredations, and its abandonment was a short and safe settlement of all complaints. Spain haughtily rejected the demand. Admiral Vernon was now commissioned, by active hostilities, to displace, eleven years after Hosier's death, the meaningless blockades. War ensued.

"There had not been," said Edmund Burke, speaking of the 18th century, "any foreign peace or war, in its origin, the fruit of popular desire, except the war with Spain in 1739. Sir Robert Walpole was forced into it by the people, inflamed by the leading politicians, by the first orators, and the greatest poets of the time. For that war Pope sung his dying notes.

For that war Johnson, in more energetic strains,
employed the voice of his early genius. For that war
Glover distinguished himself in the way in which his
muse was the most natural and happy. The crowd
readily followed the politician in the cry for a war
which threatened little bloodshed, and which promised
victories that were attended with something more than
glory. A war with Spain was a war of plunder."
The public cupidity glowed with the anticipation of
another age of buccaneers.

The verses of Glover, the author of *Leonidas*, had a
simple graphic character that took well with the popular imagination. The dead Admiral Hosier is represented rising from the glimmering wave, where Vernon's
successful ship, the Burford, lay before the conquered
Porto Bello. Addressing the living admiral, attended
by a troop of spirits—his deceased companions,—he
thus speaks :—

> " See these mournful spirits sweeping,
>   Ghastly o'er this hated wave,
> Whose wan cheeks are stained with weeping,
>   These are England's captains brave ;
> Mark their numbers, pale and horrid,
>   These were once my sailors bold ;
> Lo, each hangs his drooping forehead,
>   While his dismal tale is told.

> " I by twenty sail attended,
>   Did this Spanish town affright ;
> Nothing then its wealth defended
>   But my orders not to fight ;

57

Oh! that in this rolling ocean,
    I had cast them with disdain;
And obeyed my heart's warm motion,
    To have quell'd the pride of Spain.

" For resistance I could fear none,
    But with twenty ships had done
What thou brave and happy Vernon
    Hast achieved with six alone.
Then the Bastimentos never
    Had our foul dishonour seen,
Nor the sea the sad receiver
    Of this gallant train had been.

" Thus, like thee, proud Spain dismaying,
    And her galleons leading home,
Though condemn'd for disobeying,
    I had met a traitor's doom.
To have fall'n my country crying
    He has play'd an English part,
Had been better far than dying
    Of a griev'd and broken heart."
        *   *   *   *   *   *

In all this excitement the colonies of South America,
the mines of Mexico and Peru, were already looked upon
as acquired by conquest. " Every loud-tongued vaga-
bond in the streets of London," it was remarked in the
history of the time, " that shouted for joy, or rung the
bells in the church steeples, seemed to fancy himself a
sharer in the prey." War was proclaimed. The proclamation was greeted as a jubilee. The leaders in Parliament who had striven for the war walked in procession
after the heralds, making the proclamation by sound of

trumpet. The Prince of Wales, who had actively identified himself with the popular enthusiasm, was seen following not far in the rear of his personal friends. He stopped before the Rose Tavern at Temple-bar and drank " success to the war." Walpole, in the meantime, was muttering his sure prophecy, " they may ring the bells now, but they will soon be wringing their hands." If there was any joyousness comparable with that of the London mob, it was that of the Pretender's Court in Italy. The exiled Jacobites, notwithstanding the disasters of 1715, were secretly steeling their hearts for the outbreak of 1745. They looked upon the war with Spain as a prelude to a general one in Europe. France would unite with Spain to set King James on his throne. The time would be opportune when the fleet would be engaged in distant hostilities. The heralds of King George had scarcely finished their flourishes announcing a declaration of war, than Jacobite agents posted and galloped in all directions. In Edinburgh the zealous partizans of the House of Stuart drew up a bond of association, in which they engaged to take arms and venture their lives and fortunes for the restoration of the exiled family. They armed for fight, and the memorable field of Culloden secured an undisputed throne for ever to the House of Hanover.

CHAPTER XII.

THE declaration of war stated that "for several years unjust seizures and depredations had been carried on in the West Indies by the Spanish guarda-costas and other Spanish vessels; that great cruelties had been exercised upon the crews and the ships seized; and that the British colours had been most ignominiously insulted; that the Spanish pretentions for doing this were contrary to the law of nations, and to solemn treaties, particularly that of 1670; that Spain had made several other infractions of the treaties and conventions subsisting, particularly of that concluded in 1667, and of the convention signed the 14th of January last, by which a sum of money was stipulated to be paid before the 25th of May last, which had not been done; in consequence, general reprisals had been granted against Spain; that the Court of Spain, without publishing any order, had seized all the property of the English *in* the Spanish dominions, and ordered the persons themselves to depart *out* of the Spanish dominions, within a short limited time, contrary to the express stipulation of the treaties between the two crowns, even in case of a war actually declared:— *therefore war is declared* against the King of Spain, his vassals, and subjects." (Dated at Kensington, the 19th of October, 1739.)

Before this declaration of war had been put forth, England had issued, under date of the 10th of July, letters of marque against Spain. The stipulated

£95,000 were not forthcoming; the convention which had fixed the sum of money, and the time for paying it, had been violated; therefore His Majesty, the King of Great Britain, to vindicate the honour of his crown, and to procure satisfaction for his injured subjects, had ordered all Spanish vessels to be seized. On the 20th of August, Spain had retaliated by seizing British property wherever it could be reached, *in* or *out* of the Spanish territories.

The old buccaneer wealth flowed into Port Royal in licensed privateers. On the 23rd October, Captain Knowles, in one prize taken by the "Diamond," ship of war, had brought 120,000 dollars in hard weighed money—the *peso-duro* of common commercial phraseology. On the 5th of November, 1740, Admiral Vernon quitted his anchorage in Port Royal Harbour, with six vessels for the Spanish Main, and on the 21st Porto Bello was attacked, and the day after surrendered to the squadron. The details of the capture do not comprise many facts. It served the party purposes of Parliament to make much of it, but it was, after all, an unimportant affair. The loss suffered was *twenty men, killed and wounded,* and 10,000 dollars prize money—money received then and there by the government to pay the troops. The fortifications of Porto Bello having been blown up, the harbour was left open and defenceless. On the 24th "Chagres" was attacked, and capitulated. Every other hostile enterprise failed. Carthagena resisted. Twenty-nine vessels of the line, beside small craft, invested it. The operations against the port, and its several batteries, continued from the 4th of March, 1741, when the fleet, counting, in great and small vessels, one hundred and twenty-seven, anchored in Playagrande, to windward of Carthagena, gaining the Island of Tierra Bomba, near the Boca-chica, on the 9th. On the morning of the 26th of March, the fleet entered the harbour, fighting their way through obstructions of moored and sunken ships, and shoals; and taking forts which they held till they found the impracticability of more than partial success, when they re-embarked their troops on the 16th of May, and returned to Jamaica on the 19th. As Dr. Smollet, who was in the expedition, afterwards described it in the novel of *Roderick Random* : " nothing was heard but complaint and execration, the groans of the dying and the service of the dead; nothing was seen but objects of woe, and images of dejection. The conductors of this unfortunate expedition agreed in nothing but the expediency of a speedy retreat from the scene of misery and disgrace."

To cover the disaster by some undertaking that promised success, an attack on the city of St. Jago de Cuba was projected. The harbour Guatanamo, the old Indian name of that magnificent inlet on the south-eastern part of Cuba, called by the English since this enterprise Cumberland Harbour, was occupied by an English fleet from July to November, 1741. Troops were landed twenty miles up to be exposed to death by disease. When the force had been prodigiously diminished by sickness, the expedition returned to Jamaica.

This last calamitous exploit has nothing specially

noticeable recorded of it but the French and Spanish correspondence accidentally discovered. It revealed the concealed enmity of France. An attack had been made on a large privateer at anchor in a cove behind a rock. The vessel was taken, and the crew pursued on shore. A sailor, observing a dead Spaniard laid on an English ensign, rolled off the body, and brought the flag away, swearing no Spaniard should lie on so honourable a bed. In the corner of this ensign, obtained by such a strange accident, was found wrapped up a packet of letters. The correspondence contained the intelligence that the Marquis d'Anton's squadron, cruising to protect the French possessions, had intended to act in concert with Spain against the English; but it had been prevented, as the admiral had found that the condition of his ship was such as to oblige him hastily to return to Europe. In October of the year previous to this discovery being made, Lord Augustus Fitzroy, passing Hispaniola with four sail of ships on his way to Jamaica, had pursued four strange vessels of war that would not show their colours, and would not bring to. Night coming on, he had opened on them a running fight that lasted till daylight, when the strangers, hoisting French colours, proved to be a part of the Marquis d'Anton's squadron. The English had not hesitated to engage the ships, believing them to be Spanish, and the French had fought, desirous of a pretext to be at war, without a declaration of war. The parties, both suffering considerable loss, excused themselves to one another in the morning for the collision. The encounter, as it appeared by the correspondence found with the body of the dead Spaniard, was in furtherance of the hostilities secretly contemplated by the French admiral while England was at peace with France. The general war that succeeded for three years showed what had been anticipated by them.

Cardinal Fleury, at the head of the French Administration, had gone hand in hand with Sir Robert Walpole in maintaining uninterrupted peace. He was just dead. Sir Robert Walpole's reputation, shaken by his reluctance to go to war, when so many aggressions justified it, was irreparably gone. He retired from office when hostilities with France ensued. The time was opportune for rebellion in Scotland. James, the first Pretender, had appointed his son Charles his regent and " *alter ego.*" The House of Stuart against the House of Hanover divided British allegiance, and prepared again maritime adventurers for lawlessness.

CHAPTER XIII.

FOR twenty-seven years, under the pacific policy of Fleury and Walpole, the West Indies had endured pillage and barbarities committed by Spain. Under Spanish auspices, adventurers of all nations had taken to the profitable business of piracy, plundering every cargo under a British flag afloat. Parliament took up an inquiry into the grievances alleged. The case of Captain Jenkins was the most memorable. It clenched the determination for war by its powerful influence on the party contentions of the time.

"The poorest being that crawls on earth, contending to save itself from injustice and oppression, is an object respectable in the eyes of God and man." Burke, in making this remark, added, however, impatient contempt for the clamour of men calling for battles they were not to fight, and contending for violence they were not to feel. Jenkins' sufferings were of a kind to fill the popular mind with unmeasured execration. It was hardly possible to clothe the cruelties inflicted on him in language describing them that did not excite feelings of revenge. In touching the heart they moved the passions. His examination before the Committee of Parliament had an expressiveness that gained, on repetition, power in the public mind.

Admiral Stewart, commanding the naval force at Jamaica, had received orders in 1731 to cruize upon the Spaniards. He was to visit, without discrimination, ships, as well as look out upon the guarda-costas. The Jamaica merchants had expressed alarm at this order, with respect to merchant ships, because they knew how retaliation would be a plea for plunder, and they requested by petition the admiral to suspend the execution of that part of his instructions.

In April of that year the Bacchus, Captain Steevens, had been boarded by a guard-boat in sight of Havanna, having flying a flag with a death's head. The Bacchus made submission on being fired upon. The crew of the coastguard boarded and plundered the ship. They stripped the captain and his men, taking

away their clothes. They tortured them with thumb-
screws made from the flint-holders of their firelocks.
They burnt them with lighted matches to extort confession about their money. They learnt while inflicting
these outrages that another vessel, the Humber, Captain Rodgers, had got away from them in a night
squall, having one of their crew on board.

Somewhat in advance of the mid-year the Rebecca,
Captain Jenkins, got into their possession, homeward
bound from Jamaica. A guarda-costa boarded the
ship off Havanna. The captain was put to torture.
He was three times hung up—at one time triced up
with his cabin boy suspended to his feet. They cut
off one of his ears and departed, taking away his
instruments of navigation, and depriving him of all his
candles that he might not refer to any chart at night
for his whereabout in the Gulf stream. They reckoned
on his drifting and perishing. Being left without the
means of navigating the vessel, the Rebecca tacked
about to return to Jamaica, but the Spaniards, seeing
the ship changing its course, stood after it, and com-
pelled it to continue in the stream, declaring that if the
homeward course was not kept they would burn the
ship. Jenkins thus sailing at hazard, suffered many
perils in his voyage, but reached England, entering the
Thames on the 11th of June, though destined for
Scotland.

It was about this time that the ship of war " Adventure," Captain Lord Muskerry, arrived in England from
Jamaica with 230,000 (two hundred and thirty
thousand) dollars on board, saved out of a Spanish ship

5

of war that had been wrecked in the preceding autumn
on the Pedro shoals. This spoil, gathered from a
wreck, had set all sort of treasure-seekers on the *qui
vive* for lost galleons and sunken plate-ships. It had
been remembered how Captain Phipps, in 1687, had
enriched himself and crew with £300,000 (three hundred thousand pounds) from money got up on the silver
Cays of Puerto-plata, and how he had laid the fortunes
of the House of Mulgrave. Spaniards in the act of
recovering their bullion-cargoes when shoaled, had been
attacked and driven away and pillaged. Jenkins, it
had been asserted, was a successful actor in one of
those plunderings. A suit at law had been brought
against him in a Jamaica court to compel him to restore
specie he had carried off from a galleon wrecked on
the coast of Florida. He was a person of some family
pretensions in the colony. IIis father had died leaving
him a fortune of £500 (five hundred pounds) a-year.
In command of means he had fitted out an expedition
to make searches for wrecked treasure. It was said
that, going out with a hundred men, he had fought one
hundred and twenty Spaniards in a Cay and got into
his hands 50,000 (fifty thousand) pieces of eight. All
these occurrences were bruited when the examination
into his case was taken before the parliamentary committee. The act of pillage laid to the charge of
Jenkins was said to be the reason for torturing him
when the Spanish got him into their hands. Out of
his confession they hoped to regain their money.

Seven years had passed before this case, with
numerous others, on petitions telling of atrocious

barbarities, was inquired into by Parliament. The public mind from one end of the kingdom to the other was agitated by the horrors of licensed piracy. On the 16th of March, 1739, Jenkins was ordered to attend the House of Commons. Witnesses were examined and counsel heard. Jenkins produced his dismembered ear, dried and carefully preserved, as testimony of his barbarous treatment, adding that when he had suffered this mutilation, they told him he might carry the ear to his king, and say, when he complained, that they would serve him the same. To the question, " What were your thoughts and feelings, as a free-born Briton, when this outrage was being perpetrated? " he replied, " I recommended my soul to God, and my cause to my country." The answer had that apposition which made it current as a smart reply. The whole nation, in the repetition of it, was made to feel that the unredressed wrong was an accusation against themselves. Rarely, it was said, had an oratorical point produced such effect as this answer. It stirred the Parliament and the country into fury. Lord Pulteney declared that alliances were not necessary for the war ; Jenkins' wrongs *commanded* justice, and his single story would raise volunteers for army and navy.

Party spirit endeavoured to diminish the effect of Jenkins' case by calumniating the man. They said he had never suffered the injuries that he had described, that he had lost his ear after the fashion of Prynne and Bastwicke, of historical memory, in the pillory. It was at this time that the Earl of Mansfield, then known as Counsellor Murray, made his great reputation for eloquence. He was counsel for the petitioners to parliament. He asked for redress for what in their persons and their property were national outrages. Lord Pulteney delivered then one of his most effective speeches. The country was mad for revenge, and lost all patience when they heard Sir Robert Walpole still pleading for negotiations and pacific measures. He had carried resolutions that affirmed the Spaniards had " unjustly interfered with the freedom of navigation and commerce, and had committed depredations attended with unheard-of cruelty and barbarity;" but he merely added, further, that " reparation was due, and that the debt acknowledged had been hitherto evaded." Alderman Perry, of London, had been chairman of the committee of inquiry ; he got passed a warlike address to the throne, pledging the House to provide adequately for war if negotiations failed ; and the Lords, after expressly denying the right of search practised by the Spaniards, voted an address for war.

The popular sentiment and the popular feeling carried a resort to war. Though negotiations were pending, war was declared. Patience was exhausted. The issue of hostilities was disastrous. The glory of Porto Bello was overrated. It turned out as Walpole predicted. Those who had rung the bells were wringing their hands ; but the spirit of the nation was up against the prophet. They heard their complaints and their wrongs acknowledged, but the Ministry had delayed to strike the blow, and the result had been effectual resistance and disgrace. Glover's verses on Hosier and Vernon had produced prodigious sensation.

The wrath was universal with the failures against Carthagena and St. Jago de Cuba. On the 4th of February, 1741 (old style), Lord Sandys moved the dismissal of Walpole from the administration of affairs. After recapitulating all his shortcomings, and his corruption in office, he closed his speech, saying—" I therefore move that an humble address be presented to his Majesty, that he would be graciously pleased to remove the Right Honourable Sir Robert Walpole from his Majesty's presence and councils for ever."

Walpole, on the motion for his dismissal from office, was ordered to withdraw from the House. His conduct was under consideration, and discussion was not to be subject to restraint from deference. Mr. Wortley Montague, representing the wealth of the Commons of England, had moved the resolution for him to retire. It was seconded by Mr. Gibbon, the author of the " Decline and Fall of the Roman Empire." The precedents quoted for this proceeding were deemed harsh, and Walpole sat out the accusatory speeches, and delivered his defence. " Whatever had been," he said, " the conduct of England, he was equally arraigned. If she maintained herself in peace, and took no share in foreign transactions, the country was reproached for pusillanimity; if, on the contrary, she interfered in disputes, the Ministry were called Quixotes, and dupes of the world; if she contracted guarantees, it was asked why the nation was wantonly burthened; and if guarantees were declined, they were accused of being without allies." After going through a long and impressive speech, but less a defence than an invective, and less a reply than a cento of questions begged, he retorted on his accusers by remarking, that " if our attacks on the enemy were toq long delayed, or if they had not been so vigorous or so frequent as they ought to have been, those only were to blame who have for so many years been haranguing against standing armies, for without a sufficient number of troops we can neither defend ourselves nor offend our neighbours." Walpole, on the prorogation and dissolution of the then Parliament, about to expire by duration, retired from public life, was created Earl of Orford, the title by which his family are now of the Lords. Cardinal Fleury died in 1743, Walpole in 1745 ; and in 1748 the Peace of Aix-la-Chapelle was concluded, by which the belligerent powers engaged on all sides to make restitution of the places taken during the war. Nothing was gained, and nothing was lost.

It is curious to look into the commercial legislation of this period. When the wrongs of skipper Jenkins put the nation in a high Spanish fever, that nothing could moderate but Spanish blood, Lord Pulteney brought in a bill which, it was said, if drawn by a buccaneer, could not have more legalized their system of warfare and reprisal. It made every man a re-dresser of his own wrongs in his own way, and according to his own measure of retribution. The bill is spoken of by historians as a bill for converting the English nation into a great *Buccaneering power*. It prescribed no conditions in dealing with the property of friendly nations shipped in Spanish vessels. The French and Dutch were driving a large trade with

Spain ; the money for their goods was returned in specie in the galleons. Claimants for injuries inflicted were to keep everything they could get, and Spain was to be left to settle her accounts with those who trusted her, how she best could, for property found under the Spanish flag.

Bishop Atterbury had called Walpole, in rhyme, " the cur dog of Britain, and spaniel of Spain ;" and the party against him, when they drove him into war, required that he should show himself " fierce without fawning." The discussions went to demand as a right free-trade. Spain was to be forced to abandon her policy of excluding vessels from her colonial ports. She had recognized the colonies of other nations in what she claimed as her own seas. The colonies of Britain, in North America, had been distinctly acknowledged, but she provided by specific articles for the closure of her ports in Southern and Central America, and in the islands that made part of her dominions. No intercourse termed foreign was to be held in her empire beyond sea. Ships were not to approach Spanish coasts, but only in stress of weather, or under special licences for specific purposes. Treaties of peace, concluded by England with those conditions, were the ground on which Spain justified the visits of her guard ships, and affirmed the right of search in West Indian Seas. Her coasts swept round the whole Carribbean Ocean. The sea from the Island of Trinidad South to Porto Rico North, and along the shores of Cuba into the Gulf of Mexico, became, under her assumptions, Spanish waters.

The markets of Spanish colonies, exchanging the precious metals for commodities, were too tempting to allow of submission to this exclusive system. The merchants of Europe circumvented the prohibitions of studied devices. In 1740 Spain yielded to the necessity of providing for trade against force and fraud by her own indulgence. She introduced an important innovation into her colonial policy. Colonial trade was permitted in registered ships. Separate equipments were to be allowed, destined for the American settlements, and undertaken by individual adventurers. Ships other than the periodical fleets were to be permitted to communicate with specified ports of the colonies. Places hitherto debarred from all direct intercourse with the Mother Country were to be made ports of entry and departure under the registered licence. The registered ships were restricted to clearances from the port of Cadiz, to which port they were to return with their American cargoes; and this restriction to Cadiz alone continued until the year 1748. After that trade was allowed in other ports. The treaty of Aix-la-Chapelle, entered into on the 7th of October, 1748, amid many definite stipulations, left unmentioned the right of English subjects to navigate in those American seas, whose length and breadth Spain assumed to be her waters, without being subject to search, though that claim and the aggressions committed under it against all nations had been the reason of the war.

CHAPTER XV.

THE colonial policy of all European nations was narrowed to the close system of the Spaniards. Spanish America produced the precious metals, and wanted in exchange everything that was desirable in manufactured commodities. The exclusion of all direct trade, save under the confined liberality of the ordinances of 1740, could only be broken through by rontraband traffic. The annual ship was made a cover for prohibited trade. Bribes had effected business directly by smuggling. These were abandoned for schemes in which the merchant appeared to conform to the regulations of trade while he was breaking through them. A common device was to send a number of smaller vessels in the wake of the annual ship, allowed by Royal order specially. While the ship went into port in conformity with this permission, smaller craft that accompanied it beat about in the offing, or lay snug in some creek at a short distance, and supplied the large vessel with fresh goods over her larboard side as fast as she unloaded her original cargo over the starboard. There were other devices not so open as this. English vessels, jauntily rigged, and not exciting observation at a distance, hove to several leagues away at sea. South American smugglers, with their fast-sailing barco-longos, put off to them. Here they loaded themselves with merchandise, and sailed into their destined port, disposing of the cargo they had been supposed legitimately to have brought with them.

The people wanted merchandise; the commodities were indispensably necessary. If by other expedients they could get them as good, they could not dispose of them as cheap, when the smuggler rendered the calculations of profit uncertain. It was impossible, on a coast where distances were counted by hundreds of leagues, from port to port, to prevent contraband trade. From either shore to the Cordeliras of the Andes; from Mexico; from its Gulf stretching from Florida to Yucatan; from Panama and the coasts of Peru and Chili, English goods were to be found, as well with the uncivilized Indian as the civilized colonist. The revenue of the Government fell as the prohibitory orders against trade increased. The annual fair of Panama, where the goods licensed by Spain or directly imported by the Government were sold, dwindled away. It was no longer the great mart of South America. Merchandise was nowhere wanting, though European manufactures were admissible only in few parts. Spain felt her revenue decreasing, and instead of an open trade as the proper cure for the loss, she still sought to maintain exclusion by more repressive vigour and vigilance.

Though the Dutch commenced the depôt system in the island of Aruba, and enriched themselves by making there the depository of European goods for the Spanish market, they systematized smuggling in very effective ways beside. To gain the confidence of Spain they refused the entry of privateers into the port of Curaçoa, and they rejected all inducements for purchasing cargoes obtained under hostilities with

Spain by the allies of Holland. But they smuggled successfully. Vessels from the home-ports would bear away for Spanish America, and enter as ships in distress seeking shelter in the harbour of an ally. Leave would be obtained to unload the ship and refit. The King's officers would register the packages as they entered the government warehouse. The doors of the stores in which they were deposited would be carefully sealed. The goods were to be supposed to have remained untouched. In the night the packages would be taken out of the cases, and bales of indigo, cochineal, and even bags of bullion, would be exactly enclosed in their stead—the packages being emptied, standing as they had been arranged under seal. To enable those who had bought the goods to sell them openly, the authorities allowed a part of the cargo to be disposed of to pay the expenses of repair or refit. Forms of law were in this way made to cover unlawful importation.

It was not till after the disasters of war, and the peace of Aix-la-Chapelle, without any accommodation of differences, that England learnt the value and importance of a colonial entrepôt trade. Her neighbouring islands could be made emporiums of legitimate commerce. The great warehouses of Kingston, Jamaica, became magazines for Spanish traffic. Bullion and doubloons and dollars were brought to take away Spanish purchases in Spanish trading craft. The prohibitions of direct foreign intercourse were unalterably continued, but the intermediate system of an entrepôt was adequate and especially convenient. Guarda-costas left off their vigilance when there remained nothing afloat to look after. Spanish oppressions ceased *externally*, but in proportion as legitimate commerce gave activity to the people of the Spanish colonies, the exclusive policy which kept Creoles and natives from distinction and trust was felt *internally*, and the inhabitants sought relief in rebellion.

Through the agency of General Miranda, indirectly with France, but directly with England, the first step was taken to accomplish South American independence. The commercial restrictions had been ruinous;—the political ones were degrading. Exclusiveness designed to preserve the Sovereignty of Spain, had sown the seeds of a deep resentment only to ripen into revolt. American Spaniards, amid a mass of distinctions between Europeans and their descendants beyond the Atlantic, being shut out from all official appointments, the natives found deliverance in throwing off their allegiance. Bolivar completed the revolution that many had essayed under failure. South America was only freed when British Treaties made the revolted colonies countries of Free-trade. In 1823, the natives of America aspired to the glory of being their country's Liberators, and they achieved liberty and independence.

Jamaica mercantile houses now changed the entrepôt of Kingston for continental stores in the great maritime and interior cities of South and Central America. The intermediate commerce with this change had been reduced to little, when the American Spaniards took to direct trading with the manufacturing markets of Europe and with those of North America. The Kingston entrepôt is now extinct. Rapid communication by steam packets has made easy and ready the transit business of the Southern and Central States of the continent, and Kingston, once flourishing as a port for shipping, is limited to its own island imports and exports. Its wharves receive little goods or merchandise beyond its own immediate consumption, and though under the system of free-trade it is unrestricted in available markets for commodities, its imports, from the diminished capital employed in the staple of sugar, and the valueless character of its indigenous spice, pimento (*myotus pimento*, *L. P. vulgaris*), amount to less in each succeeding year. It throve by the gain of the few, under slavery and protecting duties; but it has lost all trading importance under competition with the many.

78

CONCLUSION.

PICAROON pillagers infested the coasts of Jamaica
till the alliance with Spain, in 1807, led to the Peninsular war. Dashes at the plantations were made to
carry away negro slaves for sale in the slave-holding
colonies. The vessels assumed the dimensions of the
large canoes which Columbus described as the state
barges of the Caciques.* In their piratical character,
the depth of these large canoes was increased by
building up the bulwarks. A single lateen-sail, spread
on a bamboo yard, ranged the whole length of the
vessel. The barco-longo—this being now the name
it bore—sailed prodigiously fast, and changed its
course without tacking. It dashed without apprehension into shoal-water; drove clean up on a sandy
beach. It could not be boarded afloat: the taffrail
being clad in raw hides kept wet, neither gave
handhold nor foothold. The manchette and the pistol
were the arms of the crew. These pillaging boats
sailed out for Jamaica, licensed from Cuba. When
the slave trade with Africa was recommenced, the
old patrons of the plundering piraguas became owners

* Washington Irving's Life and Voyages, Columbus, Vol. i., Book
VII., Chapter II. and VI. Among the Indians Jamaica surpassed
all the other islands in its maritime armaments. Every Caüque
prided himself in a large canoe, which he regarded as his ship of
state.

of slavers sailing to the coast of Africa. There is no record that one of the picaroons of a late date was ever captured.

On our beach and in our harbours may still be heard the pirate song, given in Sir Walter Scott's novel of " The Pirate," when Cleveland is carried aboard with the boat crew singing it. The natives of Kirkwall in the Orkneys heard only the first stanza:—

> " Robin Rover said to his crew
> Up with the black flag, down with the blue.
> Fire on the maintop; fire on the bow;
> Fire on the gundeck ; fire down below."

Our fisherboys do not finish the wild chorus with the words that sounded unintelligible heard in the distance by the Kirkwallers;* they end their traditional stanza with the refrain

> " Pull away, my brave boys, pull away, O!"

and continue the song with endless improvisos, such as :—

> " The prize is before us; the black flag is o'er us.
> Pull away, my brave boys, pull away, O!"

Lord Stowell, the most distinguished of all admiralty judges, after observing, there is a fashion in crimes— and in piracy, at least in its simple and original form—remarks, that " there was a time when the spirit of buccaneering approached in some degree to the spirit of chivalry in point of adventure; and the

---

* Waverley Novels, "The Pirate," Vol. ii., Chapter XII.

practice of it, particularly with respect to the commerce, and navigation, and coasts of the South American Colonies, was thought to reflect no dishonour upon distinguished Englishmen who engaged in it. The grave judge Scaliger," he adds, " observes, in a strain of rather doubtful compliment, 'nulli melius piraticam exercent quam Angli.'* England now vindicates the laws of humanity on the high seas, by making slave trading, not a breach of maritime law alone, but a violation of the law of nations—with piracy. To the penalty of a felon's death, and a felon's life servitude—in its suppression, she sacrifices more than treasure ;—she consecrates the life of her brave sailors to the generous service of human freedom. Piracy, in this form, is now an opprobrium no longer national, save in the lingering adherence to it in slave-trading by Spain.

* Lord Stowell. Adm. Judge Dodswell, 2-374.